I0476106

Cryptocurrency

─ ─ ─ ─ ─ ❧❧❧❧ ─ ─ ─ ─ ─

Bitcoin Financial History and the Future of Blockchain Technology

By Miles Price

Table Of Contents

Introduction

Congratulations for embarking on this amazing journey!

The Internet was an alien concept a few decades ago. However, the human race would be back in the dark ages without the Internet. The global change in the world of commerce promises to revolutionize the entire political and economic order.

Cryptocurrencies lie at the heart of this change. Since the Bitcoin was invented in 2008, the term "cryptocurrency" has entered our lives. This technology is here to stay and it will simply keep getting better. Cryptocurrency is cheaper, safer, faster and easier to transact with, when compared to credit cards and paper money.

The technology that will have the greatest impact on the world economy and its future is blockchain technology. Yes, you read it correctly. It is not artificial intelligence, solar energy or even self-driving car. The first wave of the digital revolution got us the Internet that was full of information.

The second wave is bringing us blockchain technology. This is the age of making use of the Internet for creating more value. It can truly transform the manner in which business is conducted and the order of human affairs as well. This ingenious protocol allows transactions to be not only anonymous but secure as well.

Blockchain is the technology that powers Bitcoin and several other digital currencies.

In this book, you will learn all there is to learn about cryptocurrency, why it is better than money, the different advantages it offers, about fractional reserve banking, the pros and cons of the federal reserve, Bitcoin and the different advantages. This learning will help you in the future as it's not just about business. It also concerns individuals, including you and may change the way you deal with money in future.

Chapter 1:

Currency vs. money

Currency and money are often used as synonyms for one another. If you look these words up in a regular thesaurus, they will indeed be listed as synonyms. However, their economic function is quite different. If you are interested in preserving your wealth, then understanding the difference between these two is vital to the equation.

Currency

For most people, currency or fiat currency, in particular, would mean hard cash or cash in hand. It includes dollars, pounds, pesos, or even yen that you can keep in your wallet or in your purse. Currency is the primary medium of exchange in a country and it could be in the form of paper or coins. Currency has been made of precious metal like gold or silver to name a few.

These precious materials were difficult to transport. The idea was to develop a form of portable currency that would serve the same purpose and was backed by these precious metals. For instance, banknotes are a type of currency that is backed by silver and gold in the United States.

These banknotes can be exchanged for legal tender at any given point of time. Legal tender means the precious metals that are used for backing such notes. The US silver certificates can be exchanged for their worth in silver. The gold standard was adopted by the US in 1879. Currency that is backed by precious metal helped in lending credibility to the issuing government.

This provided the necessary trust for making these currency systems work. People accepted this currency system since they knew their wealth was secured by the precious metals backing it.

Gold Standard

President Roosevelt and the Congress, in the year 1933, started to take the US off the gold standard. This disabled the citizens of US from demanding the payment for their currency in gold. The public was also required to transfer all the gold coin, gold bullion and gold certificates held by them to the Federal Reserve at a pre-determined price of $20.67 per ounce.

This price was later increased to $35 per ounce of gold. The Federal government could regulate the money in circulation since it was holding as well as controlling all the gold. During the period of Roosevelt's administration, inflation was created in order to stimulate the economy. The irony of this situation is that the gold standard was done away with for building the confidence of the public in the economic system.

President Nixon, in the year 1971, announced that the US would no longer convert dollars to gold at the price of $35 per ounce, and the gold standard was abandoned altogether. US citizens were thus introduced to the system of fiat currency that is backed by nothing other than their trust in the government.

Money

Money is also known as commodity money and it can be any kind of commodity, ranging from seashells to stone. This can serve as a medium of exchange for buying and selling goods, services and also for debt payment. Unlike the fiat currency that is issued and decreed by the government, gold and silver have an intrinsic value.

Precious metals are valuable due to their scarcity. Unlike the fiat currency that can be printed at the government's whim, precious metals are finite. Gold is absolute, unlike fiat currencies. These metals can neither be created nor destroyed. Only their shape can be changed. This would exist forever. Try applying this same concept to the paper money that you have in your wallet. For many years, gold and silver have duly served us as money because of their special features.

Removing the currencies from this has led to the detachment of our faith from their value and this has allowed governments, as well as financial institutions, to alter their value according to their whim. Fiat currencies are transient, and their value depends on the rise or fall of their nations, unlike gold and silver that will stay the same.

Chapter 2:

Fractional Reserve Banking

History

The story that's generally told about the origin of fractional reserve banking is quite interesting. It is said that goldsmiths used to store precious metals in their vaults and people would go to them for storing any of their precious metals as well. Over a period of time, gold smiths realized that they could capitalize on this opportunity.

They could lend this gold out and make an investment with it, they could keep the profit that they earn from it and then return the same into the vault before anyone could get to know.

Well, do you really think this is how banking came into being? Well, probably not and history wouldn't definitely support this. However, this is a useful story. It reminds us that the resources that simply lie around in a vault aren't of much value.

Putting these resources to work will help in making a productive investment, you can earn a profit out of this and even the community would benefit from this.

Chapter 2: Fractional Reserve Banking

The next question that you might have would be, why should you learn the workings of fractional reserve banking in the first place? There are some nations that do better than most other nations. One of the causes for this would be that the nations that can provide a better environment for making a good investment grow faster. The environment in this context could include the laws that govern property rights, laws about taxation and even their trade policy.

These factors are all good for the accumulation of capital and for making an investment. This is what banking is all about. It is better to think that banking has come out of a need for investment instead of thinking that it came out of all the gold that was sitting in the goldsmith's vault.

You will have a better understanding when you are aware of the need and the problem that is being solved by banking.

Are banks necessary for making an investment? Perhaps not. Direct finances do take place in many economies and especially in the US, direct finance is an important part of the banking system. Direct finance is the scenario where an individual would lend money to a corporation by either buying their stocks, bonds, or any other form of security.

These funds would in turn be used by the corporation for its expansion, growth and for paying a rate of return. A significant portion of American investments is funded through banks. Banks help in channeling funds to not just huge corporations, but to small business and even households too.

So, what are these institutions that help in funneling money to the investors referred to as? These institutions are banks. The term bank has got such a narrow meaning. You will need to think about all the different financial intermediaries that are involved too.

Let us take a look at the institutions that accept funds from different savers and then identify useful investments for investing such funds. Why do all these financial institutions exist and what are the problems that they are trying to solve that cannot be solved by direct financing?

The problem is referred to as asymmetric information by economists. You would naturally want to lend money to a person, who would pay back your capital with interest on it, wouldn't you? Then how do you decide that the person has got a good investment opportunity waiting for him? What's the guarantee that they will fulfill their obligations? Financial intermediaries help in providing this sort of information.

They help in distinguishing between what a good and a bad loan would be. Once the loan has been given, they help in monitoring the behavior of the borrower so that they can get back their funds.

This is quite a difficult undertaking, and banks do this for free.

Would a financial crisis cast a shadow on the ability of the financial intermediaries of picking a good loan? And their ability to monitor that the investment would be repaid? When you think about it, the problem of the crisis that has only recently passed is the exception to this rule.

However, from the perspective of banks, the manner in which the problem regarding asymmetric information is solved makes two things clear. The first one is that the standards had been reduced. This implies that banks were no longer relying on the information that they had received about particular borrowers and also that they weren't making an effective use of the money that they had.

These loans were then being collated and then sold to others. This means that these loans were no longer on the balance sheet of the bank and they weren't necessarily monitoring these loans closely.

This is what the world has witnessed. These financial institutions somehow got away from their basic function. They were no longer solving the problem of asymmetric information as cautiously as they once used to. When they didn't perform this function, the problems followed.

These are certain broad reasons why it is important to understand the workings of fractional reserve banking and also about financial intermediation.

The workings of Fractional Reserve Banking

There are certain reasons why it is really important for people to comprehend the different processes of fractional reserve banking. A lot of the "money" that economists refer to is generated from this process. You can think that money has two origins.

The first one would date back to the times when economists used to refer to it as "outside money" and sometimes as "central bank money" or "base money." This refers to the currency or perhaps the reserves that have been created by the Central Bank and is referred to as the Federal Reserve and it links into the financial system.

It is also referred to as base money since the financial system rests on top of this and this helps in generating a different type of money that is referred to as "deposit money."

Deposit money is also referred to as inside money. It is the money that has been generated through fractional reserve banking. Banks accept a deposit, then they loan it out, the loan would become another deposit and this deposit, in turn, would become another loan, and so on. This process keeps continuing.

Through financial intermediation, that is the process of lending and deposits and more lending and deposits, a new type of money is created and it rests on top of the base money. This money is referred to as inside money.

You will need to comprehend the process through which banks help in turning credits to loans to understand two things. The first one is to get a hang of what we refer to as money in an economy. The second one is for understanding the effect that different policies of the Central Bank would have on the supply of money.

A monetary policy has different tools and each of these tools is designed for controlling the quantity of money that is in circulation in the economy. These tools function mainly through the banking system.

For instance, the Federal Reserve is capable of changing the reserve requirements and of also forcing the banks into holding more or even less as reserves within their vaults. This help is either increasing or reducing the creation of inside money. For instance, if the Federal Reserve was to lower its reserve requirements, this would allow all the banks under its authority to start lending out extra money.

This would, in turn, create additional deposits, which allows the fractional reserve banking system to pump more money into circulation in the economy.

However, on the other hand, if the central bank were to increase the requirements for the reserves to be maintained by banks, then the supply of money in the economy would be curtailed or reduced.

Outside money or base money would be put into circulation through the Federal Reserve and through the banking system by the purchase and sale of securities in the open market. The Federal Reserve is capable of altering the amount of base money that should be in the economy.

On top of this, the entire financial system can be made use of for expanding loans and for the creation of more deposits through the process of fractional reserve banking. From a technical point of view, it is important to understand this particular process if you are really inclined towards understanding the different tools that the central bank makes use of.

The monetary policy is usually conducted within the United States through the system of open market operations. When you buy or sell the securities that have been issued by the US government in the open market, this either increases or decreases the reserves that are maintained in the banking system.

If you purchase the securities offered for sale by the US government in the open market, then you would be freeing up its reserves into the financial system. This would then, in turn, be converted into further loans and deposits that keep on multiplying.

Of course, this process would work in reverse as well. Supposing the public decides to withdraw all their deposits from the financial intermediaries. These deposits would have been given out as different forms of investments. There can be different problems regarding liquidity that could plague the financial system.

This is one of the main duties for which the Federal Reserve was created. The Federal Reserve would be the lender of the last resort. This would ensure that banks always had a market for selling the assets for marinating the necessary reserves that would be required for paying off all the depositors in times of crisis.

Importance of Fractional Reserve Banking

One of the most important uses that fractional reserving banking offers is that it helps in the pooling of savings. It helps in gathering small savings and then provides an opportunity to lend the same to different markets catering to big as well as small enterprises. It provides borrowing options to households as well.

Businesses that need funds, corporations that require an additional inflow of cash can always make use of this. The primary advantage of banking and of financial institutions, in general, is that they help in making available funds that most of us don't have, that would be considered to be too expensive for most of us.

One of the main reasons why the story about goldsmiths would be appealing is because one of the common misconceptions people have is that the money that you deposit in a bank just sits there idly. You will definitely be receiving interest on the money deposited. However, did you ever wonder where this interest comes from?

When you really think about this, the bank is investing the money that you deposited with it, and the profits from these proceeds are given to the customers as interest. Your money isn't lying idle in a vault somewhere; it is actually doing some work.

Chapter 3:

Shakiness of Fiat Paper Money

All throughout history, there have been different schemes that have been made use of for producing currencies that cost nothing for their production. These currencies don't have any survival value whatsoever and what value they do have is substituted for commodity money.

Artificial money is referred to as fiat money and it has a value for the simple reason that it has been declared to be valuable by either the central bank or the government. Fiat currency schemes help in replacing the survival value of the commodity money that has a subjective value and this can be substituted as a medium of exchange.

Modern currencies like the US dollar, British pound, euro, or even the Japanese yen are all forms of fiat currency. A fiat currency is a unit that is worth what it can purchase and it doesn't have a set standard that can be made use of for measuring its value. Its value cannot be measured since its purchasing power isn't stable. There are different problems that fiat currencies have.

There isn't a spoon

Have you seen the really popular movie "The Matrix"? In this movie, the protagonist is Neo. There's a particular scene in which Neo has a conversation with a gifted child who is capable of bending spoons by using his mind. In this scene, the child tells Neo that he shouldn't focus on bending the spoon and must simply understand it. The truth is that there is no spoon and it is only yourself that you will have to bend.

In a similar fashion, there's a difference between what an abstraction is and what an abstract is. Money is an abstraction in the same manner in which a container would encompass both bottle and a jar. Abstractions are certain facets of language that help in describing the world.

On the other hand, an abstract is the mental representation of a particular idea like liberty for instance. Abstract concepts are nothing more than ideas that exist within the human mind. Law, for instance, talks about the concept of justice but then again, an arbitrary law isn't just simply because it is a law. Unjust laws do exist.

Simply making a declaration that a stone is a seafaring vessel wouldn't give it the ability to float on water. If it has got sufficient momentum and spin, then it can perhaps skip on the surface of the water, but that's about it. An absurdity of similar manner underlies the concept of fiat money.

Money is an abstraction and value is an abstract concept. Fiat money, on its own, has got no value.

Coercion

Coercion is a characteristic feature of fiat money. Most people wouldn't accept this unless they had been forced to do so. In the United States, for instance, the gold standard was replaced by making use of legal force. US citizens were compelled to accept the irredeemable Federal Reserve Notes instead of the gold certificates with the threat of incurring a penalty of either $10,000 or ten years in prison, or even both.

Rent seeking

The schemes of fiat currency have been designed for extracting rent by forcing the conduct of commerce in the system of fiat currency. Human beings trade with one another for their survival. Their ability to be able to exchange value for value is as natural as their right to life, liberty, and the pursuit of happiness.

In a marketplace that is based upon voluntary arrangements, there would be no middlemen trying to extract any form of economic rent in exchange for their said permission to engage in commerce.

Immorality

Schemes of fiat currency are considered to be immoral since the primary factor that makes them acceptable in the first place is coercion. Making people forcibly accept artificial money that doesn't have any value of its own against their will is indeed an immoral act.

Added to this, the schemes of fiat currency put all the control in the hands of those who can control the currency. This means that wealth would be redistributed by simply altering its availability, its quantity, and also the distribution of the currency.

Central planning

Fiat currencies are based on coercive relationships instead of voluntary relationships; the central authority has got the power of eliminating other competing currencies and for establishing a monopoly. Central economic planning isn't just anti-democratic; it is bound to fail at some point in time. Human society isn't blessed with infallible individuals who can take financial and economic decisions on behalf of everyone.

Take the example of the USSR. Central planning in an economy would produce a perennial stream of unintentional consequences that would, in turn, lead to more interventions. This would in turn simply destroy the whole of the economic activity.

Instability

Fiat currencies have got no direct relationship with the survival requirements of human life. They require insignificant physical input of an economic nature. Since the central planners get to decide all this, the quantity of a fiat currency scheme is usually incorrect.

This, in turn, causes instability in prices and causes artificial depression in the economy regarding the production and distribution of money. Price stability can never be achieved while following the fiat currency system.

Economic volatility

Fiat currencies are usually loosely coupled with physical economic activity in the real world. Due to this, they tend to become decoupled and eventually they will become untethered over a period of time.

An economy is the sum of millions of independent human beings and there is no possible way that all those responsible for fiat currency can guess the required quantity of fiat currency. However, they are capable of recognizing the wrong quantity by the resulting consequences. These could include a credit boom, depression, recession, and even economic collapses.

The Great Depression had in fact set in 16 years after the US Federal System was established. Economies can be volatile for multiple reasons. Fiat currencies usually end up magnifying this economic volatility further.

Debasement of currency

Voltaire said that paper money would go back to its original intrinsic value that is zero. Fiat currencies are all issued by governments or different central banks. This currency represents intangible concepts like that of faith and credit. However, a fiat currency on its own has got no lasting value.

Fiat currencies have an inherent tendency of decreasing their own purchase power over a period of time as more and more currency is being produced – more so in systems based on fractional reserve banking and debt-based schemes of fiat currency. In the debt-based schemes of fiat currency, the currency will need to be either inflated or deflated and, if not, the system would collapse.

All those responsible for the currency would end up producing more than what is necessary for marinating a stable price or for sustaining stability in economic activities. Price instability and even economic volatility would be the result of this. The debased value of currency would ultimately undermine the entire economic framework of that particular society.

Redistribution of wealth

Increasing the amount of currency in the economy will simply distort the distribution of money and it will redistribute the purchasing power, effectively stealing wealth from a major chunk of the population for serving the interests of the privileged few. Redistribution of wealth, as opposed to the production of more wealth, will simply cause a net loss of wealth in society.

The government deficit spending, though motivated by good purpose, will change the quantity of currency and will result in the debasement of the currency. The government deficit spending operates in a dishonest fashion and comes with a hidden tax on all the savers and wage earners.

Concentration of wealth

Over a period of time, the fiat currency schemes will help in the accrual of wealth and property in the hands of those who are privileged to be able to create currency. This will, in turn, increase the concentration of wealth in society. From a political and economic point of view, excess concentration of wealth in an economy would be destabilizing.

An individual who has got a million dollars in his pocket wouldn't buy as many consumer products, cars, or appliances as ten households that have got an income of a hundred thousand dollars.

Moral hazard

Power has the tendency to corrupt and absolute power leads to absolute corruption. Fiat currencies are created as a result of monetary monopolies like loans, they help in obtaining something for virtually no cost. As a result of this, those who are responsible for the creation of fiat currencies would enjoy great influence over the economic as well as political backdrop.

Human beings can never be good caretakers of a currency system that would provide one section of society with all the means for obtaining something for absolutely nothing. In fact, all those societies that are dominated by the immoral schemes of fiat currency would eventually develop a something for nothing pattern – a culture of entitlement; where everyone would be focused on living at the expense of the other instead of focusing on the creation of wealth.

Corruption

A moral hazard of fiat currencies is that they encourage cronyism and corruption. This would ultimately lead to a culture that is infested with corruption. Who will be responsible for keeping an eye on those who are supposed to be the guardians? History is ridden with the multiple horrors of absolute power and with instances of monetary abuses that result in the collapse of an economy.

Democide has been the leading cause of death in the last ten decades. Fiat currencies are good at increasing the poverty quotient in the society. These systems help in redistributing the wealth in such a manner that they create a wealthy minority that doesn't produce wealth in any manner.

Confidence failure

Since the value of the fiat currencies is predominantly subjective, being able to maintain the perception of having a certain value when there is an economic decline regardless of the increasing prices is an uphill battle. Fiat currencies are dependent on the confidence and trust that the public has in those who are responsible for that system.

When a system of fiat currency has been abused, then the confidence of the population in it would also fail and it would simply revert back to its original intrinsic value. The intrinsic value is zero. A monetary policy based on the fiat currency system would concentrate on maintaining the confidence of the public. Behavioral economics, for instance, has become an extremely important tool for the implementation of economic and monetary policies.

As a result of this, the economic reporting that was given by the government, central banks, and media would not be objective. Management of various perceptions has the effect of being able to influence the subjective state of all those who would use the fiat currency for maintaining its perceived value. Perception management at its best is one sided and in the worst case it is nothing but propaganda.

Counterparty risk

The value of the fiat currencies depends on the trust in the counterparties. Trust, just like confidence, is an abstract notion and it is purely subjective. In the world that is objective, all the agreements between the governments and the various central banks, and all those that rely on the different schemes of fiat currency can be modified as well as broken accordingly.

In fact, they are usually broken whenever a currency has been debased. All the promises of broken governments and failed banks would render all this money worthless.

Transaction settlement

A transaction that would take place in commodity money would be a direct exchange of value for something of value. When a transaction in fiat currency is performed, one part would hold fiat currency and the other one would be the recipient of all the merchandises or services.

This is a backdated violation of the contract, as the value of the currency can differ, and it can become zero at times. There will always be a residual third party in the transaction. This would be the central bank or the government and the transactions would stay unsettled.

Chapter 4:

Dollars and Bitcoins

Are fiat currencies and Bitcoins the same thing? Let us try and answer this question in this chapter.

Lionel Trilling said that even though human beings have invented money, they make use of it, they don't really understand it. It has got its own set of laws and it has got a life of its own that cannot be controlled.

The answer to the question posed earlier would be quite obvious to all those who can understand the manner in which currency works. However, for all those who are still trying to understand all this, read on. There is nothing called too much knowledge, right?

For all those who don't know much about money, apart from it being in paper form or coins, and your love for it, you are in for a surprise.

Let us start off by changing your perception of paper currency. All money is referred to as fiat money. You might wonder who is responsible for determining its value. Well, we are the ones responsible. Long ago, there was not much difference between fiat currency and the digital Bitcoin.

This was the time when the US dollar and various other global currencies were still based upon the Gold Standard. The Gold Standard was commodity based and its underlying principle was that every dollar or unit of currency in circulation should be backed up by a pre-decided amount of gold bullion (this is the commodity) that would be held in a reserve.

Now you might be wondering who in fact decided the worth of all this gold. The answer yet again would be "we did." This meant that the power that we once held was taken away. The sad thing about all this is that most of the public never realized that this took place.

At a point of time, there was a lot of controversy and mistrust that was linked with the Gold Standard. It was during the 70's that it was learned that there were more US dollars in circulation all around the globe than the amount of gold that was held in the Fort Knox for backing the currency.

This is when the US government decided to do away with the monetary standard. Other countries followed the example set by the US. So, if you are amongst those that still believe that Fort Knox backs your dollars, you need to think again. It does not and it has not done so in over four decades. In a way, this is a good thing.

The current state of Fort Knox is riddled with controversy. It is supposedly said to be the biggest facility housing gold but there are so many conspiracy theories about the amount of gold that is actually held in it, the public is quite worried about the state of the US dollar.

Chapter 4: Dollars and Bitcoins

Now that you have understood that all the dollars in your pocket aren't anything but mere paper currency and not a promissory gold notes, you will definitely start thinking better about Bitcoin.

Now that you understand that there is no commodity based paper money, it is not too hard to realize that fiat currency and Bitcoin aren't very different except for one difference, a huge difference.

Fiat currencies and Bitcoin are quite similar at their very core. This isn't quite that simple though. This one difference makes Bitcoins more appealing and promising.

The main difference with the Bitcoin is that it is cryptocurrency. Cryptocurrency is a digital medium of exchange, unlike paper money. It is first of its kind, and it perhaps the only form of global currency that is free from any form of intervention from government or regulations.

The value of money isn't determined randomly. It has been assigned a value by the government of the world. Most of this value is based on the US dollar and the present global standard helps in determining the value of all the other currencies.

The USD is considered to be strong since the United States is presumed to be the strongest economy in the world. This is the reason why its money is influenced by different global perceptions regarding the states and their current events like wars, the balance of trade, credit balance, the reputation of its president, policies, taxes, laws, spending, etc.

The USD, the so-called global currency standard, has got more to do with the way it is perceived rather than the commodities that are responsible for driving it. In reality, it is just fiat money and nothing more than that. By now you will have realized that there indeed is a huge difference between Bitcoin and fiat money.

Bitcoin represents the hope that one day we will be able to take back what was taken from us way back in the 70's, the Gold Standard. This is a fiat form of currency but in fact it is a peer-to-peer financial system.

You will be in control of how much it is actually worth. You might be wondering if it would be silly to purchase or make use of Bitcoins that don't have any value. Bitcoin when they had started out in the year 2013 were valued at around $13 per coin, they are valued at about $550 per coin today. In November 2013, these coins were valued at $1200!

The rate of these coins is quite volatile. There is a fixed cap on the number of coins that are available; therefore, there is only a small chance that inflation would destroy this value. The future does seem quite interesting when you think of it. If you are still not sure about Bitcoins, you don't immediately have to invest in them.

They did have quite a strong run in 2013, but they are extremely volatile. You will learn more about Bitcoins in the coming chapter.

Chapter 5:

Federal Reserve

The Federal Reserve is also known as Fed, informally. This is the central banking system of the US that was started by Congress in 1913. The Federal Reserve Act was signed by President Woodrow Wilson in order to provide the country with a financial and a monetary system that would be more stable and flexible.

The creation of this law was a response to all the financial panics that kept taking place one after the other. Since the time of its implementation, the roles and responsibilities of the Fed have been steadily increasing. Its structure has definitely evolved and it has been understood that it is essential for creating a stable economy. There are also many people who believe that the Fed does more harm than good. In this chapter, let us take a look at the pros and cons of the Federal Reserve.

The benefits of the Federal Reserve

Helped in establishing a national currency

Before the Federal Reserve System was initiated, there were different types of currencies that were made use of in the US. After this, there was only one common currency that was to be used throughout the country and it helped in the smooth functioning of the economy.

Increases transparency and predictability

This rule-based system that is used in the monetary policy of the Federal Reserve helps in increasing the predictability as well as the transparency of the actions taken. This, in turn, helps the Central Bank in explaining its actions to the general public and in helping the market predict what the Fed could do.

This has a significant effect on the lives of people like low rates of interest that would be suitable for debtors instead of the creditors. The market observers would also know the plans of the Fed and perform accordingly to save their time and money.

A sound financial system

The Federal Reserve System helps in the conduct of the monetary policy of the country by influencing the credit and the money conditions in the economy for ensuring full employment and stability in prices as well. In addition, it helps in regulating and supervising banks and several other financial institutions for making sure that the financial system will protect the rights of the consumer in the country.

Financial interests are represented

Without the presence of such a system, banks would showcase the interests of the country and it would not be the best option available since these intuitions are more concerned about the private sector instead of the public one. In addition, the Fed would need the banks to subject themselves to an external and an impartial audit.

If this system didn't exist, then all the audits would be internal ones and this can lead to corruption.

Helps in increasing the credibility

By setting out rules, the Fed is able to reduce the incentive to renege the promises later on. Without any rules, it is believed that the central bank would be able to keep inflation low, but it might get tempted to print more money in order to generate additional income for the government.

Contain the systemic risk

The Federal Reserve works for marinating the financial stability of the country and for containing the systemic risk that would come about in the financial markets in the country.

In addition, it also helps in providing financial services to the government and other institutions in the United States as well as several other foreign financial institutions. Apart from all this, it helps in overseeing and operating the payments mechanisms in the country.

Disadvantages of the Federal Reserve

Invasive and unconstitutional

The Federal Reserve System has been regarded as being anti-capitalism. The finances are controlled by government organizations instead of private businesses. This means that there would be an increase in the size of the government and hence has been criticized by many.

Created for enslaving the government with debt

The US economy can go into debt only if it wants to. Most people usually speculate that the government would simply print as much money as it wants for paying off all the debts of the government. However, this wouldn't be allowed under the Fed system. The US government is not the authority that is issuing the currency but it is the Federal Reserve.

Thus, it is referred to as Federal Reserve notes. Whenever the government would want to create more money, then it would simply have to go into debt.

Favors private interests over public interests

It is believed that the private interests and the lobby groups tend to have a great deal of influence over the Fed. This would allow individuals to benefit rather than the society as a whole. The Fed is a government institution, but it is still run by individuals who are business minded and this would open up doors for corruption to seep in.

Utility and validity isn't universally accepted

The constitutionality of having a national bank has been a part of debates all around the world, to such an extent that the federal government can control and plan the economy making use of that bank.

Throughout the history of the Central Bank, there's been a lot of negative talk about the policies that it has implemented. Some people even believe that the monetary policy of the country is so tight that it is resulting in unemployment.

It will increase stability

Contrary to the contrary belief, the Fed has alleviated bank panics. However, many people believe that the central bank cannot manage the monetary policy of the country and that it is increasing the instability.

Some believe that it is quite accommodative to the political administration; others believe that it is interfering too much in the economy.

Manipulates the US economy

It has got the power to increase or decrease the rates of interest and it can, therefore, speed up or hinder growth.

It can also inflate the economy and then let it pop. Most American citizens tend to blame the president on the performance of the economy; these leaders don't really have much control over the economy when compared to the Federal Reserve.

In order to get a good opinion on whether the Federal Reserve System in the US is beneficial or not, you would need to weigh in all the pros and cons listed above.

Chapter 6:

Benefits of Cryptocurrency

The strength of the cryptocurrency lies in its simplicity of being able to transact, the lack of middlemen, and has no government interference. Over the last few years, cryptocurrency has been gaining a lot of property. In the initial phase, it seemed as scary as the credit card did to its users in the initial days of credit cards becoming available. You might have heard terms like Bitcoin or ether.

These are types of cryptocurrencies that make use of blockchain technology for keeping it safe and secure. At present, there are different types of cryptocurrencies that are available and a quick Google search will tell you all about it. Once the cryptocurrency becomes stable, there would be little scope for either inflation or deflation. In this chapter, let us take a look at the different benefits that cryptocurrency has got to offer.

Scam

Cryptocurrencies are digital in nature and they cannot be forged. Not just that, they cannot be reversed arbitrarily by the sender just like the charge backs on the credit card.

Instant settlement

Purchasing real property involves a few third parties (like lawyers or notary), delays, and also the payment of a fee. Bitcoin or cryptocurrency can be thought of as a large database of property rights. Bitcoin contracts can be designed and then enforced to either eliminate or add the approvals of a third party, any reference to external facts, or it should be completed at a date in the future for a fraction of the expense and the time that is required for the completion of the traditional asset transfer.

Lower fees

There is no transaction fee that is levied on cryptocurrency exchange since the miners are already compensated by the network. Even though there is no transaction fee, most would expect that the users would make use of a third party service like Coinbase for the creation and the maintenance of their Bitcoin folders.

These services are similar to PayPal and provide the online exchange system for Bitcoins and are likely to charge a user fee. PayPal neither accepts nor transfers Bitcoins.

Identity theft

When you give your credit card to a vendor or a merchant, then you will be giving them access to your credit line, regardless of the quantum of the transaction. Credit cards usually operate on what is referred to as pull basis. This means that once the store has initiated the payment, then the assigned amount would be automatically pulled from your concerned account.

Cryptocurrency, on the other hand, makes use of a push technique. This would mean that the holder of the cryptocurrency could send exactly the amount that the holder would want to give to the merchant.

Access to everyone

There are more than 2.2 billion people out there who have got access to the Internet or even mobile phones but don't have access to the traditional exchange. Such people are the ones that are suited for cryptocurrency. M-PESA is a mobile-based service that helps in transferring money and also in micro financing.

This service has also announced a Bitcoin device and now one in every three Kenyans has got a Bitcoin wallet.

Decentralization

A huge network of computers all over the world makes use of blockchain technology for managing the Bitcoin database and the transactions. A network, not a single authority, controls Bitcoin. Decentralization in here would signify that the network would operate on a peer-to-peer basis or a user-to-user basis. This helps in forming collaboration instead of a controlling authority.

Universal recognition

Cryptocurrencies aren't bound by exchange or interest rates; they don't have any transaction fees or any other charges applicable in any country. This makes them suitable for international usage without having to face any problems.

Chapter 6: Benefits of Cryptocurrency

This will in turn help in saving time and money for conducting business, instead of having to spend hours, for transferring money from one country to another. It can operate at an international level and can be used with ease.

There isn't an electronic cash system that you can make use of wherein your account wouldn't be owned by a third party. For instance, take the example of PayPal. If the company has decided that your account has been or is being misused for any reason, then it has got the power to freeze all of your assets without having to consult you.

It is then your responsibility to get it all cleared up for regaining access to your funds. When you use cryptocurrency, you will have a private key that would have a corresponding public key that would make up the address of your cryptocurrency. This cannot be taken away from you unless you lose it on your own.

Cryptocurrency has got a long road ahead of itself before it is capable of replacing traditional forms of currency and credit cards before being accepted as the global commerce tool.

Most people are still unaware of how cryptocurrency works or what cryptocurrency is. They will need to be educated about all this before they can apply it. Businesses will have to start accepting it and they will need to make it simpler for signing up and getting started with this.

Cryptocurrency will help you have complete control over your money and it is quite secure. When made use of in a proper manner, it will be a force to be reckoned with. It will definitely change the global commerce map.

Chapter 7:

The Inception Of Bitcoin

Bitcoin is a type of digital cash; it is generated and held in an electronic form. No one has got any control over this. Unlike paper currency, these Bitcoins aren't printed and they are produced by people and different businesses that have electronic operations around the world but, makes use of software that helps in solving mathematical problems.

This is the first instance of the upcoming group of money that is referred to as cryptocurrency.

How is it different?

Bitcoin is used for buying things electronically. In this sense, they are quite similar to the conventional fiat currencies like the dollars, or euros that are digitally traded as well.

The most important characteristic of the Bitcoin and the one thing that makes it different from regular money is that it is decentralized. There is no single institution that is capable of controlling the network of Bitcoins. This would appeal to some people since their money isn't under the mercy of a large bank.

Who created it?

Satoshi Nakamoto, a software developer had proposed the idea of a Bitcoin. This was an electronic system of payment that was based on mathematical equations. The idea behind this was to create a form of currency that would be completely independent of a central authority while still being transferable electronically instantly and with a low transacting cost.

Who would print it?

Well, no one would have to print it. Since this isn't printed in a physical form by a central bank, it is unaccountable to the population and has got its own set of rules. Banks in general, are capable of producing more money for covering their national debt and this would devalue their currency. Instead, Bitcoin is digitally created when the community mine them and anyone is free to join. Bitcoin is mined by making use of a distributed network. This network also helps in processing transactions that can be made with virtual currency and make Bitcoin its own network of payments.

Can you create unlimited Bitcoins?

In a contradictory way, yes! But also no. The rules that govern the workings of a Bitcoin say that about 21 million Bitcoins can be mined by the miners. These coins can be divided further. The smallest part of a Bitcoin, which is the one hundredth millionth part of a Bitcoin, is referred to as Satoshi, after its creator.

What is it based on?

The conventional currency used to be based on gold or silver or any other precious metal. Theoretically, it was true that if you handed over a dollar, you would be entitled to getting that dollar's worth in gold. However, the Bitcoin is not based on gold and it is based on mathematical equations. Across the globe, people are making use of software programs for following a particular mathematical equation for generating Bitcoins.

This formula can be checked by anyone online and it is available free of cost. This software is an open source and this means that anyone will be able to take a look at it to make sure that it is doing exactly what it was programmed for.

Characteristics of a Bitcoin

Let us take a look at the several features of a Bitcoin that set it apart from fiat currencies.

The Bitcoin is decentralized. This means that one particular authority does not control it. Every machine that can mine Bitcoin and processes these transactions would become a part of this network. All the machines will work together. Theoretically, this means that one particular authority does not have the power to take away people's Bitcoin.

Even if a part of the network happens to go offline due to some reason, money will still keep on flowing in. All the conventional banks have got a multistage procedure for opening a bank account. Setting up the merchant accounts is another long and tiresome procedure. When it comes to Bitcoin, you can set up your Bitcoin address in no time and without the payment of any fees. It is kind of anonymous as well.

Users are allowed to have multiple Bitcoin addresses and these addresses aren't linked to any names, addresses, or any other personal information. The functioning of the Bitcoins is completely transparent. Every transaction that takes place is stored in the network in a ledger format and this is referred to as the blockchain. Blockchain says it all. If your Bitcoin address is public then anyone will be able to tell the number of Bitcoins that are stored at that address.

However, they wouldn't know to whom the address belongs. There are different measures that you can take for making your activities more protected on the Bitcoin network. Any bank would charge a transaction fee for any international transaction. However, the Bitcoin doesn't do so. You will also be able to transfer money anywhere in the world and the receiver would receive it within moments.

The Bitcoin network processes transactions rather quickly. Once you have sent Bitcoin out of your account, there is no way that you will get them back. If the recipient sends them back then you can get them. If not, they are gone forever.

It does seem like Bitcoin has got a lot going for it, doesn't it? How does it all work in practice, though? You will learn more about Bitcoins in the coming sections.

How are Bitcoins mined?

In the traditional system of fiat money, governments are responsible for printing money as and when they need it. However, when it comes to Bitcoins, they cannot be printed. Bitcoins are discovered. Computers across the globe will mine for these Bitcoins by competing against one another. People keep making use of the Bitcoin network for sending Bitcoins to one another across the world.

Unless and until someone actually keeps a track of who is sending what to whom, no one will be aware of all these transactions. The Bitcoin network would deal with this all by collecting the data regarding all the transactions that were conducted during a set period into a list.

This list is referred to as a block. It is the job of the miner to confirm all such transactions and then write them in a ledger. This ledger comprises of a list of blocks and this list is referred to as the blockchain. This can be made use of for exploring any particular transaction that could have taken place between two Bitcoin addresses.

When a new list of transactions is created, it will be added on to the blockchain. It will, in turn, create a lengthy list of transactions that took place in the Bitcoin network. An updated copy of a block would be given to everyone who participates in it, so they will be aware of what is going on.

However, can you always trust this ledger and is all of this held in digital format? How do you make sure that this blockchain will stay intact and it is not tampered with? This is the point where the "miners" come into the picture.

When a block of transactions has been created, then the miners will put it through a particular process. They will take the information that is present in a block and apply the mathematical formula or equation to it for turning it into something different. The result would be a shorter sequence of letters and numbers that seem random and this is referred to as a hash.

This hash would be stored in the block at the end of a blockchain.

These hashes have got a couple of interesting properties. It is really easy to create a hash from all the data that is present in the blockchain. However, it is impossible to find out what the original data was by looking at the hash. It is easy to produce a hash from huge amounts of data; each hash is unique in itself. If you change even one character in the block of Bitcoin, then the hash will change too.

Miners not only make use of the transactions present in a block for generating the hash, they make use of other bits of data as well. One such piece of data would be the hash of the previous block of Bitcoin from the blockchain.

Since the hash of each block is produced by making use of the hash from the previous block in the blockchain, this forms a digital wax seal. This provides the confirmation that the particular block, and every other block after it is legal and it has not been tampered with. If it has been tampered with, then the others would know about it.

If you try and fake a transaction by changing the block that is stored within the blockchain, then the hash of that block would change as well. If someone were to check the legitimacy of the transactions in the blockchain by running it through the hashing equation, then the fake block will be spotted instantly. Since the hash of every block is made use of for producing the hash of the subsequent block in the chain, simply tampering with the hash of one would result in the subsequent hash going wrong as well.

This would continue until the very end of the chain and all the blocks will be tampered with.

How to compete for coins

This is the manner in which a block is sealed off by the miners. They all tend to compete with each other for doing this. There is specific software that is written for just mining these blocks. Every time someone has managed to create a hash, such a person will receive 25 Bitcoins.

The blockchain will be updated and everyone that is present on the network will also hear about this. This is the incentive that will keep the miners mining for more. This problem with this is that it is easy to produce a hash from the collection of all the data that is available. Computers are extremely good at this. The Bitcoin network will have to make this slightly more difficult. If not, everyone would be simply hashing multiple

Bitcoin blocks and all the Bitcoin that are available will be mined in no time. The Bitcoin protocol has been designed in such a way that it makes this simple process more difficult by making use of something referred to as "proof of work."

This protocol will not simply accept any old hash. It has certain criteria that need to be met. The hash of a block needs to look in a specific way and it needs to contain a specific number of zeroes at the beginning. There is no particular way in which you can determine the way a hash will look before it is produced.

As and when you include newer pieces of data to the existing mix, the hash will look different too. Miners are not allowed to interfere with any of the existing data transactions in a block. They should, however, change the manner in which they were making use of the existing data for creating a hash. They do this by making use of a random piece of data that is referred to as a nonce. Nonce is used in a transaction for creating a hash.

If the hash isn't fitting into the specified format, then the nonce will be changed and the whole thing will be hashed again.

It usually takes multiple attempts for finding the nonce that suits your requirements and all the other miners on the network will also be trying to the exact same thing.

Chapter 8:

Mtgox.com

MtGox fell prey to a flaw in the Bitcoin which, coupled with other things, was the reason for the downfall of the company. Let us take a look at the MtGox story. The story behind the downfall of MtGox is nothing short of it being unbelievable. How could a business not notice that more than £200 million worth of assets had just vanished? The answer to this was a small flaw that existed in the Bitcoin.

This was further aggravated by the protocols and internal practices at MtGox. Due to all this, they ended up creating a harmful situation wherein an attacker could easily convince the company to hand over their assets or money without even realizing what it was doing.

At the crux of the MtGox problem, the issue was found to be in the Bitcoin and it is referred to as transaction malleability. Whenever a Bitcoin transaction has been made, then the account that is sending the money will include the important information within the Bitcoin that is being sent. It includes the information like who is sending it, where it is coming from, or where it is going.

Every transaction has got a unique transaction ID. However, some of the data that has been made use of for generating this ID might come from that part of the transaction that is insecure and unassigned. As a result of this, the transaction can be altered.

Nothing would be lost in such a case since the important information regarding payment is signed securely. However, this can cause problems from the sender's end.

In the case of MtGox, the site was expecting certain transactions to show up in a public ledger under a particular transaction ID that was recorded. When these transactions didn't show up, since the thief had edited the transaction ID, the thief could then make a complaint saying the transaction failed and the system would retry and then initiate a second transaction and send out Bitcoins again.

Malleability in transactions is a flaw that exists within Bitcoins and it wasn't MtGox's fault. The transactions were simply renamed and they couldn't discover it. This flaw was discovered in 2011, and it could have been made harmless by making use of software that would report such imbalances in transactions.

The issues with malleability cannot indeed be fixed overnight, but they can be dealt with and the burden of doing so would lie on the company that is engaged in Bitcoin transactions. However, just the fact that some Bitcoins were stolen wouldn't lead to the kind of collapse that MtGox witnessed.

It is alleged that MtGox never even conducted a single audit of all the customer deposits it received. The CEO of MtGox, Mark Karpeles, would probably be the only one on the inside who would know how the cold storage of this exchange could be trapped.

It is still unclear how this particular type of storage leak happened over a period of time without anyone getting wind of it. One of the main questions posed by the fallout was how long was this company operating with insufficient funds for paying off all their depositors. The issue of transaction malleability was discovered in 2011, and then it is safe to assume that these thefts would have also started around then.

The actual trouble for MtGox started in 2013 when the company had to suspend the withdrawals in US dollars for a period of two weeks. Customers started taking away their money and Bitcoins from the company because of this. This went on for a while until eventually there were no Bitcoin deposits in the company.

It held about 2000 Bitcoins during the starting stage of this crisis whereas the customer deposits were over 600,000 Bitcoins. In the month of February, it had to suspend their Bitcoin withdrawals. There was a meeting conducted later on in which it was demanded that the CEO of the company and his colleagues come clean about what had happened and the loss incurred by the company was notified to the Bitcoin foundation.

On 23rd February 2013, Mark Karpeles resigned and the MtGox website was closed shortly afterward.

Chapter 9:

Fintech

The phrase Fintech is being increasingly used in the fields of media and technology. Despite it being the "in" thing, it is a term that not many have understood fully. This indeed is a fresh term and has not yet been featured in the Oxford dictionary's online version.

The importance of it cannot be ignored. One thing that it isn't is a buzzword. Fintech is the area that is drastically changing the world that we live in and the manner in which business is being conducted.

Fintech is typically applied to that segment of the business that is messing with sectors like the ones responsible for mobile payments, transfer of money, loans, and even the management of assets. One of the reports from Accenture had found that the global investments in Fintech have increased from $930 million in the year 2008 to more than $12 billion in the beginning of the year 2015.

The highest rate of growth was witnessed in Europe in the year 2014. This figure will keep on growing in the coming years due to new innovations, development in financial regulations, change in customer behavior and other related factors. The financial sector in the UK is the main reason for the recovery of the country after the global meltdown.

Why Fintech matters

Fintech has changed the manner in which companies do their business. The conventional business turning towards the local high street bank or a traditional bank is not the only option that is available to businesses. Whether it is crowd sourcing or mobile payments, entrepreneurs are spoiled for choice.

It has never been any cheaper or easier to set up your business or even expand it further. For instance, crowd sourcing as its name suggests allows individuals to collect funding for their ideas from anyone residing anywhere. You no longer need to meet people to get them excited about your idea. You simply pitch your idea on the Internet and if it appeals to the audience, funds will start coming in.

Transferring money across borders is no longer a headache and it can be done instantly. You can make use of TransferWise for sending money across the borders as easily as conducting any domestic transactions. Even small firms and individuals will be able to transfer money easily and it isn't expensive. These are just a few ways in which Fintech has managed to make business easy and also lower the cost of operations.

Smartphones have indeed changed the game completely. The always-online culture has given people access to loads of information and data that they were never able to access before. They can do this from anywhere. Whether you want to check your online account or set up an investment portfolio, you can easily handle all your financial affairs without any difficulty.

Chapter 9: Fintech

Fintech is only getting started. There are unlimited possibilities that will open up for businesses. There will be a complete change in the way business is conducted.

Conclusion

I would like to thank you once again for purchasing this book.

In this book, you learned about the difference between money and currency, all about fractional reserve banking, the origin of Bitcoin, the disadvantages of fiat currency, the pros and cons of Bitcoin and Federal Reserve, and the rise and fall of different websites that deal with cryptocurrency. This book is a beginner's guide to getting a hang of what cryptocurrency is all about.

By now, the terms Bitcoin, cryptocurrencies, blockchain technology, and fractional reserve banking will no longer seem intimidating. Cryptocurrency is here to stay and it is quite beneficial. It overcomes all the disadvantages that fiat money poses. Learning about cryptocurrency will help you in making the most of your investments and help you make better financial choices as well.

Lastly if you enjoyed this book, it would be much appreciated if you could leave a review on Amazon. The best way for this book to make its way into the hands of more readers is through truthful reviews about this work. Please write what you liked about this book and what could be improved upon. Any and all feedback is helpful as I continue to serve the needs of my readership.

Thank you and all the best!

www.ingramcontent.com/pod-product-compliance
Lightning Source LLC
Chambersburg PA
CBHW071820170526
45167CB00003B/1381